KATIE COURIC

Table of Contents

Chapter 1

From Morning to Evening to Web

The Television Hall of Fame got its start in 1984, a place for major TV stars to be recognized for extraordinary careers of information, entertainment, or both. The organization behind the hall of fame says this award is presented to "person who have made outstanding contributions in the arts, sciences, or management of television, based on either cumulative contributions and achievements or a singular contribution of achievement."

The first year the Hall of Fame was inaugurated, it celebrated the careers of the likes of Lucille Ball and David Sarnoff. Later, the entire original cast of Saturday Night Live was inducted.

To contribute to the world of television on such a scale is no small matter. These entertainers or informers often make great sacrifices to please their audiences. Morning show hosts must be up extremely early, making an everyday social life nearly impossible. Evening broadcasters are often tied up behind the scenes preparing their segments, only to stay up late into the night appearing on live television.

Actors in scripted television must keep nearly impossible hours when their series are filming. And, in this more modern age of an ever-critical audience, even the personal lives of many television stars and news broadcasters are on display. A moment of poor judgment at home can cut a career short.

In 2016, four leading US news broadcast networks, ABC, CBS, FOX, and NBC, were honored with a special variant of the award—Hall of Fame Cornerstone."

And yet, years before that, in 2004, one new broadcast veteran and morning show host was awarded a place in Television Hall of Fame long before her comrades in the news business. That person was Katie Couric.

A Versatile News Anchor

Couric's career has taken her through nearly every major news organization in the United States, including ABC, CNN, NBC, *60 Minutes*,

CBS, then back to ABC, and finally to Yahoo! News. In that time, she has interviewed celebrities, politicians, criminals, victims of harassment, and prominent government officials.

Serving as a host of the Today Show for 15 years, Couric received the label of "America's Sweetheart."

When Couric was inducted into the Television Hall of Fame, she had been hosting the Today Show for more than a decade during much of the 1990s. And yet, even at that point, her career was only about to blossom and move in completely new directions. Leaving NBC, she started work for the CBS Evening News. During her time with CBS, she contributed a few times a year to the journalistic program *60 Minutes*. One of her most notable interviews with *60 Minutes* was her chat with Captain Chesley Sullenberger after the miraculous landing of a passenger plane in the Hudson River. She would later play herself in the movie Sully, reenacting that very interview across from Hollywood superstar Tom Hanks.

Couric also became very well known for her series of interviews of Republican Vice-Presidential nominee Sarah Palin, interviews that were replayed multiple times on national television during the time leading up to the 2008 presidential elections.

Katie Couric's versatility shows in her willing transition from the television broadcast medium to web shows, first with the show @katiecouric from 2009 to 2011, then, later, with Yahoo! News.

For a couple of years, Couric had her own talk show, Katie, which aired under the Disney—ABC Television Group and aired weekdays in the middle of the afternoon (right after General Hospital on most local ABC stations).

So from small-time reporting to co-hosting a national morning show to national evening news to a talk show and web shows, we have seen Katie Couric continue to vary and transition her broadcast career through the years.

Beyond TV—Books and Film

Couric is the author of two children's books, a collection of essays, and, more recently, a tell-all memoir, entitled *Going There*, which has made quite a few waves for its irreverent treatment of big names in television.

In addition to appearing in front of the cameras, Couric has also been hard at work behind the scenes, acting as executive producer for a number of films and documentaries. For example, she produced and narrated the documentary *Fed Up* in 2014, which explored the food industry and the plague of obesity in the US. Two years later, she also produced and narrated *Under the Gun*, an exploration of gun violence and gun control. She also produced several documentaries for National Geographic and even a Lifetime drama.

Chapter 2

Early Life

Katherine Anne Couric was born on January 7, 1957, in Arlington, Virginia. Her father, John Martin Couric, Jr, was a public relations executive and news editor for The Atlanta Journal-Constitution and the United Press in Washington, DC. He had attended the nearby University of Virginia as a young man and had stayed in the area of Arlington his whole life. Couric's mother, Elinor Tullie Henne, worked as a part-time writer while caring for the family home.

Arlington, Virginia—at the Very Heart of Our Nation

Arlington is technically a county in the state of Virginia. It has no city, and yet it is one of the highest populated counties in Virginia. Within the county are the Pentagon, Reagon National Airport, and Arlington National Cemetery. This county was once considered part of the District of Columbia, then named Alexandria. Because the county touches Washington DC, it is considered part of the Washington metropolitan area.

The history of Arlington County goes all the way back to the British Colony of Virginia. The area was then considered part of Fairfax County. After the United States won its independence, George Washington designated the nation's capital to include the area of Arlington as the southernmost part of DC. Years later, retrocession legislation was passed to bring the area back under the control of the state of Virginia instead of the national capital.

During the American Civil War, Virginia seceded from the Union, although the northernmost part of the state was never really under Confederate control, being just across the river from DC.

Years after the city of Alexandria separated from Alexandria County, the county was renamed the modern Arlington. This prevented a great deal of confusion.

Throughout the 20th and 21st centuries, the area of Arlington has grown considerably, proving to be the perfect area for many who work in the DC area to live and commute to work.

School Years and Early News Experience

Katie Couric attended public schools in Arlington--Jamestown Elementary, Williamsburg Middle School, and Yorktown High School. She was a cheerleader in high school, and she also got her first taste of news reporting at the time, working as an intern at the radio station WAVA.

WAVA (or WAVA-FM) got its start as WARL and WARL-FM. The AM station broadcast only during the day, but the FM sister station continued to broadcast into the night, even though most Americans did not have radios equipped with FM receivers in those days. When the United States Transdynamics Corporation acquired the stations in 1960, the call sign was changed to WAVA.

In the 1970's WAVA, serving the Washington DC area, made the transition to an all-news outfit. In fact, WAVA-FM was one of the only all-news FM stations at the time. This was the same time that Katie Couric started working as an intern there.

One can imagine the amount of work an al-news station had to do at that time. There was no sophisticated AP news stream at that time, and digital search options were non-existent. And yet WAVA served as a source of 24-hour news for years, until, in 1977, the station was sold and became a Rock station.

University of Virginia and Newspaper Work

Couric followed in her father's footsteps by attending the University of Virginia in 1975. UVA was founded by Thomas Jefferson in 1819 and has been a central part of our nation's education system ever since. Famous students that attended this university include Edgar Allan Poe.

Couric was a member of the Delta Delta Delta Sorority. She also worked for the university's daily newspaper, The Cavalier Daily.

The University of Virginia in the 1970s was undergoing a notable change. Prior to 1970, neither women nor African American students were allowed. This change meant a major shift in the culture and community of the university throughout the '70s. During this time, several female students took up prominent positions in the daily newspaper.

For several years, The Cavalier Daily was seen as too left-leaning, so much so that a competing newspaper went into publication. However, as funding declined in later years, only one newspaper would continue, and the Cavalier won out.

During her senior year at UVA, Couric was granted the great honor of serving as senior resident of The Lawn, a small, exclusive residential area at the heart of Thomas Jefferson's Academical Village. Couric graduated in 1979 with a bachelor's degree in American Studies.

Immediately upon leaving school, she found work working for one news organization after another, starting her award-winning career as a broadcaster and television host.

Chapter 3

Early Career

In 1979, the recent university graduate Katie Couric was looking for work in the news. It did not take her long to find what she wanted. First, ABC News hired her for their Washington DC bureau. Later, she also worked as an assignment editor for CNN.

In 1984, she started work for WTVJ in Miami, Florida as a general-assignment reporter.

WTVJ was the first television station to sign on in the state of Florida, getting its start in 1949. In its early years, it was affiliated with CBS (making a switch to NBC in 1989), although it carried programming from various major broadcast networks for decades.

In 1983, Wometco founder and president Mitchell Wolfson died, leaving behind a family that had no interest in continuing the broadcast empire that included WTVJ. In 1984, the company Kohlberg Kravis Roberts & Co. bought out Wometco for a billion dollars, making it the largest corporate buyout in history up to that time.

It was during this tumultuous time that Couric started working as a reporter for WTVJ. This Florida station was not very stable, though, so when the opportunity to move back to DC and work for the NBC-owned WRC-TV, she took it. She worked for that station for the following two years.

WRC-TV has been around since 1954. In 1987, when Couric started working as an on-air reporter for the station, it was using the evening news brand Channel 4 News, or, more simply, News 4. It featured both a daily 5:00 PM news segment and a 6:00 PM Friday news program.

On WRC-TV, Couric earned both an Associated Press award and an Emmy for her reporting work during those two years, from 1987 to 1989.

Working for NBC News
In 1989, Couric joined NBC News, making the jump from the smaller NBC-owned-and-operated WRC-TV to a much larger audience. She served as Deputy Pentagon Correspondent. The

Pentagon, remember, was conveniently located in her home county of Arlington.

NBC News, the news division for NBC Universal, presides over what is now America's number-one-rated newscast, NBC Nightly News. It also includes the longest-running television series in US history, Meet the Press.

The history of news television is intimately tied to the history of NBC since the first regularly scheduled US television news broadcast was a creation of NBC News. On February 21, 1940, Lowell Thomas, a radio news broadcaster, sat before a television camera as he read his script for the network radio broadcast. This television broadcast was technically a simulcast, and it was only viewable for residents of New York.

From those simple beginnings, a long-standing tradition of television news broadcasting began. NBC News was also responsible for a program called The Was As It Happens, which reported on the final days of World War II. NBC News also reported live regarding the 1948 presidential election, in which Harry S. Truman won over New York governor Thomas E. Dewey.

By the early 1960s, NBC News had over 700 correspondents and cameramen, many of whom were stationed around the world. Unfortunately, the news program began to lose both funding and viewers over the next couple of decades. The program NBC Nightly News would begin to revive the network's news chops, however. The battle was slow and challenging, but by the mid-199's NBC Nightly News once again started to take first place in viewership across the nation.

In the late '80s, when Katie Couric started working for NBC, the network was still struggling to gain a stronger viewership. As a result, Couric saw many opportunities to show her skills during this time.

In addition to working as the deputy pentagon correspondent, Couric also jumped at every chance to substitute for better positions and get more screen time. These sub opportunities mainly presented themselves during morning programs, such as Today, Sunday Today, and NBC News as Sunrise. At times, she substituted as host or co-host of Today, or even as anchor or co-anchor for both Today and News at Sunrise.

This airtime gave Katie many opportunities to show her charm and professionalism in the morning show and morning news atmosphere. It is evident that the corporate big-wigs at NBC saw that in her, as well, because, in 1991, she was offered the opportunity to substitute Norville for an extended period. After all, Norville was on maternity leave. When Norville decided not to return, Couric was offered the position of co-host permanently.

Chapter 4

The Today Show

The Today Show, or simply Today, first aired way back in January of 1952. It was the first of its kind, a morning talk show, a show that would air daily in the morning, including news, the weather, special interest pieces, profiles of celebrities, and other light-hearted entertainment.

Originally, Today aired only on weekdays from 7 to 9 AM. In 1987, its programming expanded to include Sundays. In 1992, it even included Saturdays, as well. The Today Show was so popular that the midweek program expanded from two hours a day to three hours a day in the year 2000, and then it was expanded once again to a daily four-hour program in 2007. For years, being the only morning show of its kind, Today maintained the top viewership in the US for its time slot. Over the years, Today has battled with Good Morning America, owned by ABC for the number one slot. Today and GMA have switched back and forth for the number one and number two slots.

Signing On as Permanent Co-Host
When it was revealed that Norville would not be returning to The Today Show, Katie Couric, who had been filling in as a substitute co-host during Norville's maternity leave, was announced as the new permanent co-host. This announcement came on April 5, 1991.

Of course, as we have seen, Couric was no stranger to the show at that time. She had filled in for Bryant Gumbel as host of Today before. She had also filled in for Jane Pauley and Deborah Norville as co-anchor in the past. She had even appeared as a substitute for the Sunday edition of Today, and she had also served as the political correspondent for Today since she started working for NBC back in 1989.

Because both Today staff and audience members were used to seeing Couric on the show, it was an easy transition for her to take on the co-host role permanently.

Today's Origin Story and History
Sylvester Weaver, a veteran of advertising during the golden age of radio, had been hired in

1949 by NBC to take on the long-standing programming lead CBS had at the time. NBC needed to change things up to attract new viewers. What would Weaver come up with?

Weaver was instrumental in the creation of shows like both The Today Show and The Tonight Show. Weaver's philosophy was that great TV could inform as well as entertain. Until that time, there was a clear line between a show that was informative (such as the news) and an entertaining show (such as a comedy sketch show or sitcom). But why could a show not do both?

While still in production, The Today Show had the tentative title of The Rise and Shine Revue. Fortunately, the more catchy title of Today was adopted before the show made it to the air.

Following Weaver's original concept, Today blended national news headlines and interviews with lighter interest pieces and gimmicks, including the recurring presence of a Chimpanzee on the set during the show's early years.

The idea of a morning show would spread worldwide, making the idea of breakfast-time news and variety show something of a staple for many television and radio networks around the world. To this day, The Today Show continues to be the original and longest-running morning talk show in the world. It has stood the test of time, unlike CBS' The Early Show, which managed to last from 1999 to 2012—a noteworthy achievement of its own.

The first host of Today, Dave Garroway, was 39 years old when the first episode aired live for the Eastern and Central time zones. He hosted Today for nine years. During the later years of his tenure, the show went from a live format to pre-recorded format. The show was recorded the previous afternoon, and then the tapes were played the following morning. Today went back to a live format in 1961 when Garroway left the show, and John Chancellor took over as host.

Since then, Today has shown live for the Eastern and Central time zones, then on a delay for the following US time zones. At pre-set times during the show, there are four-minute slots allowed for local cut-ins. At 26 and 56 minutes past every hour, local affiliate stations can show local news, weather, traffic reports, and local advertising during these periods.

Today in Recent Years—Going Digital

The Today mobile app was released in August of 2013 - the first advancement into modern digital broadcasting.

Later, in June of 2014, a satellite radio simulcast was put out through SiriusXM. This was part of Channel 108, Today Show Radio. Other than a live simulcast during the usual morning time, the channel would also include highlight reels entitled The Best of Today. So far, this more digital version of the show is only available in the United States, being blocked from Canadian subscribers of the SiriusXM satellite radio services.

Couric and NBC's Other Programming

During the same decade-and-a-half that Couric worked as a co-host of Today, she also worked on various other shows for NBC, including starting an evening weekly TV news magazine program called Now with Tom Brokaw and Katie Couric in 1994. The evening program faired well, although it was later folded into part of the much larger Dateline NBC show.

Dateline originally started in 1992, airing on Tuesdays with co-anchors Stone Phillips and Jane Pauley. Because Dateline was increasingly popular, Now with Tom Brokaw and Katie Couric was rebranded as Dateline Wednesday. As Dateline grew in popularity, more days were added, including Fridays and Mondays. Eventually, it peaked at six days a week. Later, Dateline gradually was reduced in the number of days as audiences were getting tired of the legal reality TV genre.

This strategy of "stripping" show days and times has been very successful for NBC. While viewer interest gradually waned when it was on air several times a week, the network reduced the number of days, adding public interest in the days that it continued to air on. NBC would later use the same strategy of "stripping" with other programs like The Jay Leno Show.

Couric would continue to give news reports on Dateline regularly. She would also appear regularly on NBC Nightly News, the weekend edition of NBC Nightly News, as well as various special occasions, such as the Olympics and the annual Macy's Thanksgiving Day Parade. In fact, she hosted NBC's coverage of the parade for 14 years in a row, from 1991 to 2005.

Couric also worked on several one-time news specials, such as Everybody's Business:

America's Children from 1995 and Harry Potter: Behind the Magic in 2001.

On April 5, 2006, Couric announced that she would be leaving Today after 15 years. Later that same day, it was announced that Couric would start working for CBS.

Chapter 5

CBS Evening News

CBS is short for Columbia Broadcasting System, which was the name it was known by from 1928, when it was first established, until 1974. From then on, the transition was complete, and the company was universally known (and now officially titled) CBS.

When Katie Couric joined CBS in 2006, she was given a salary so large that it made her the highest-paid journalist worldwide. Why was CBS so desperate to hire her? In order to understand this, we have to go back to the humble origins of the company and then see the situation CBS was facing in the mid-2000s.

CBS in Radio Broadcasting

Before there was a Columbia Broadcasting System, there was the United Independent Broadcaster Network in Chicago. Arthur Judson, a talent agent from New York City, formed it, and yet, almost from the very start, the venture was drowning financially and needed more investors. This is when the Columbia Phonograph Company, the manufacturing company behind Columbia Records, came to the rescue. So, by April of 1927, the United Independent Broadcaster Network had been renamed the Columbia Phonographic Broadcasting System.

Even with the injection of funds from Columbia Phonograph, the broadcasting system was having serious trouble staying in the green financially. Columbia Phonograph wanted out, so they sold to a small group of private investors, who, in turn, handed over the day-to-day work of running the company to a wealthy, brilliant young man named William S. Paley.

If there is a real superhero to this story, it is Paley who saved CBS before it ever really even took off. One of his first acts was to rename the company to a more streamlined "Columbia Broadcasting System." It is ironic that the company that contributed to the "Columbia" moniker, Columbia Phonograph, did not stay around, and yet their legacy lives on to this day.

Paley was the son of a cigar family from Philadelphia, and he was related (by marriage) to the new owners of the company. One thing

Paley knew about radio from his family's cigar business was this: radio ads sell products! Moreover, he knew radio advertising was the way of the future, making this broadcasting system brimming with potential profit. In fact, his faith in radio was so strong that he brought up enough of the company to become the 51% shareowner in 1928.

In his first year as president and largest shareowner, Paley began to turn CBS around. First, he purchased the station WABC (no relation to the current WABC), located in Manhattan. In order to make this purchase pay for itself, he began lining up affiliates and advertisers. He also found a partner in Adolph Zukor of Paramount Pictures. Paramount was looking to get into broadcast radio.

In the days of the '20s and 30s, long before televisions were in people's homes, the major movie production studios were looking for a way to getting entertainment into the homes of moviegoers. The obvious move was to buy up (or partner with) radio affiliates and networks. Later, they would move on to tv, and, today, in the age of the Streaming Wars, we see companies like Paramount, Disney, and HBO, looking to expand to subscription-based streaming companies to gain additional revenue and build a brand with people that now spend much more time in front of mobile devices than their TV and the radio combined.

But at this time, radio was the new frontier of at-home entertainment. Families listened to the radio together in the evenings, be it live broadcasts of orchestra performances, famous singers (the likes of Frank Sinatra), comedians, adventures serials (like Superman and the Shadow), the news, and—of course—ball games.

In September of 1929, Paramount acquired 49% of CBS, making Paley and the studio partners. The relationship between CBS and Paramount continues to this day. CBS was nearly renamed Paramount Radio, but when the stock market crash in 1929 made Paley nervous, he decided to hold onto whatever brand equity CBS had already made with listeners across the country.

In order to really solidify CBS as a major contender, Paley dedicated himself to forming strong relationships with affiliates when other broadcasting companies, like NBC, would charge smaller affiliates to run certain forms of programming—those programs not directly sponsored by some product of the company—Paley took a different approach. He gave away any program that was not sponsored for free. In fact, in some cases, he would actually pay small affiliates to pay them. As a result, CBS grew much larger than any other broadcasting network at the time.

Paley's successful run at CBS was grounded in much more than his excellent business sense. As his friends and colleagues would describe it, he also had "a gift of the gods, an ear totally pure." In other words, he had the ability to spot high-quality entertainment on the spot. So he would find and hire the best entertainers, the smoothest voices, and the most engaging personalities. He found and signed deals with the likes of Jack Benny and Bing Crosby.

CBS had a varied entertainment lineup for each evening, including music, comedy, and variety shows. Then, in 1930, CBS found itself in the prime position to broadcast news through the radio airwaves, as well.

CBS News—Even During the Time of Radio

On April 21, 1930, Ohio Penitentiary found itself amid a heartbreaking tragedy. A fire broke out inside the prison. As one inmate would later describe it, "There was nothing to do but scream for God to open the doors. And when the doors didn't open, all that was left was to stand still and let the fire burn the meat off and hope it wouldn't be too long about it."

Even as the smoke entered the inmates' cells during this devastating event, many guards refused to let inmates free. As a result, 322 inmates were killed in the fire, and another 230 were hospitalized. During the fire, some inmates managed to overpower a guard and get ahold of his keys. They set about releasing fellow prisoners so they could escape. This led to a riot as escaping inmates attacked firefighters who arrived on the scene.

In the midst of this horror, a prison that called itself "the Deacon" established a telephone connection with CBS, allowing him to give a live description of events live on national radio. This was the first taste of what new broadcasting on the radio could be like. CBS officials would later call it a "shocking journalistic coup."

Nevertheless, even with this idea of news and radio combining, it took time for the idea to produce consistent fruitage. Four years later, in

1934, there was still no regularly scheduled new program on any nationally affiliated radio network. The problem was with sponsors. Many sponsors did not have any interest in their ad money going to new programs. And who could blame them? Would a homemaker listening to an unsavory or tragic news program feel better about the soap ad being read directly after the depressing news reading? Wouldn't that negatively impact the soap's branding? Sponsors that did like the idea of advertising during news programs expected veto rights over news topics, something no radio company would allow.

Another combatant in the progress of broadcast news was the newspapers, which viewed radio as a direct competitor. So they did all they could to stall the introduction of news to the radio.

Despite the obstacles, Paley was insistent that radio and news would become soulmates. In the fall of 1934, he launched an independent new division of CBS. The idea of reading fresh news on-air was completely new, but CBS was the first to tackle this challenge consistently. People became so accustomed to listening to new reports on the radio that, in 1938, a dramatized adaptation of War of the Worlds (the book by

H.G. Wells) unintentionally convinced many Americans that aliens were actually invading the United States.

The Jump from Radio to Television

In 1946, there were about 6,000 televisions sets in operation in the US, most of which were in the area of New York City. There were already three stations in the city area at that time. By 1949, there were approximately 3 million sets in the country, and, by 1951, that number had risen to 12 million. While CBS managed to beat out NBC as the highest radio network in the nation, the 1940s were scary for radio executives, who were not sure how television would affect their business models.

Companies like CBS and NBS needed to expand to TV or go extinct. So they made the leap.

In the mid-1940s CBS performed a talent raid on NBC radio, sniping out some of the best performers. These would become stars on CBS radio and television. One somewhat-known actress and radio star on CBS refused to transition her show "My Favorite Husband" to television unless her actual husband would be cast in the correct role. In 1951, that is how we got *I Love Lucy,* which immediately became a TV sensation.

For decades, CBS was at the top or near it, thanks in no small part to amazingly successful shows like *I Love Lucy.* The world-famous "eye" logo became well known, and Americans trusted CBS above all other networks.

In the mid-to-late '80s, however, this would all start to change.

The Fall of CBS—and the Fight Back Up

When NBC started to air hit shows like *Miami Vice* and *The Cosby Show,* CBS began to fall in the ratings big time.

Throughout the 1990s, the "golden age of television," CBS battled against NBC, ABS, and TBS for ratings. While CBS released some top-rated programs like *Diagnosis Murder, Walker, Texas Ranger,* and gained exclusive rights for Major League Baseball games, other networks were putting out their own hits. Viewers we left with hard choices regarding what to watch. The prevalence of the VCR in the 90s made it easy for views to record their favorite shows, too, and simply fast-forward through the commercials, making it harder to get more ad money from wise sponsors.

During the early 2000s CBS was desperately climbing back to the top. Reality TV made a splash, and CBS released shows like *Survivor* and *Big Brother*, which became smash summer hits for the network. The 2000s also saw the rise of a new wave of police shows with a twist. CBS put out shows like *Cold Case*, *Without a Trace*, *Criminal Minds*, and *NCIS*. New-millennia sit-coms were big for the networks as well, the likes of *Two and a Half Men*, *How I Met Your Mother*, and *The Big Bang Theory.*

And yet, through this, Fox was a newcomer on the rise, with a smash hit like *American Idol.* At the same time, NBC was on the rise in the area of news broadcasting. So, in the increasingly competitive atmosphere of the time, CBS was desperate to inject new lifeblood into both its drama programming and its new broadcasting.

And this is where Katie Couric came into the picture.

Couric and CBS's Desperate Attempt to Beat NBC at the News

In 2006, when CBS sniped Couric from The Today Show, CBS was desperately trying to beat NBC at the evening news game. Couric at this time was a big name in both variety "infotainment" television, such as mornings shows, but also had a strong flare for serious reporting as a political and pentagon correspondent. She has also already gained the title of being America's Sweetheart.

When CBS hired Couric, they signed her on with a $15 million contract, making her the highest-paid journalist around the globe at the time, right up there with ABC's Barbara Walters. On September 5, 2006, Evening News with Katie Couric aired for the first time.

CBS had paid a lot of money for Couric to be the lead anchor and managing editor of their new flagship evening news program. They hoped to revive the evening news format, which had taken back seat bother thanks to more aggressive scripted and reality TV shows and the emergence of 24-hour news and weather channels (such as CNN and the Weather Channel), which rose quickly in popularity after 9-11 and the following war in Afghanistan.

On that first broadcast featuring Couric on September 5, 2006, new graphics packages and sets were also introduced, along with a new theme composed by Academy Award-winning composer James Horner. Other CBS programs, such as *Up to the Minutes*, *CBS Morning News*, and *The Early Show*, also received theme and graphics makeovers at the same time, unifying CBS' big push to boost ratings. The opening title sequence featured the voice of Walter Cronkite, a legend in new broadcast culture.

Couric's rating was a significant improvement over her predecessor. However, it soon became apparent that the program was not going to take the number one spot. CBS Evening News trailed behind both ABC World News and NBC Nightly News in ratings.

Despite the lackluster return in ratings, the show was award-winning, gaining Couric and CBS Evening news the Edward Rm Murrow Award for best newscast. In 2009, Couric also won the Emmy Governor's Award for her overall broadcasting career, which would have been in no small part thanks to her jump from morning variety television to evening news broadcast.

While working for CBS, Couric also contributed to another award-winning program: *60 Minutes*, discussed in the following chapter.

Chapter 6

60 Minutes

It was the morning of January 15, 2009, and US Airways Flight 1549 was in trouble.

The Airbus A320 had only been in the air a few minutes, taking off from New York City's La Guardia Airport, en route to Charlotte, North Carolina, when the plane hit a large flock of Canadian geese. These large birds, suffering a tragedy of their own, no doubt, caused a complete failure in both of the plane's large jet engine turbines. The plane was gliding through the air, right over New York, with no propulsion.

Within seconds, the pilots, Chesley "Sully" Sullenberger and Jeffrey Skiles realized they were quickly running out of both altitude and options. Sully immediately initiated an engine restart sequence, just to see if the engines might come back, while also turning on the auxiliary power unit. Next came the call to air traffic control:

"This is Cactus 1549. Hit birds. We have lost thrust on both engines. We are turning back towards LaGuardia."

By the time the controller offered a runway for them to perform an emergency landing, Sully knew that would not be an option. "We may end up in the Hudson," the pilot said, referring, of course, to the Hudson River. The possibility of Teterboro in New Jersey was discussed, but it was also ruled out as a possibility. Finally, the pilot said they would be in the Hudson since it was the only option he saw available to him.

A few seconds later, Sully announced to the 150 passengers and 3 flight attendants: "Brace for impact." A few heartbeats later, the jet engine made an unpowered water landing in the icy cold Hudson River.

Miraculously, every human soul on the plane survived. They were able to get out of the slowly sinking aircraft and be rescued by emergency services boats that rushed up to provide assistance.

Like many newspapers, online news organizations, and all television news networks, CBS provided minute-by-minute news coverage of the accident and aftermath. Katie Couric was there, as well, interviewing and informing the public.

Couric Covering the Miracle on the Hudson

Within hours of the event, the phrase "Miracle on the Hudson" was coined, and that moniker has stuck down to this day regarding the emergency water landing of Flight 1549.

That night, Katie Couric was on the cold streets of New York, interviewing passengers and others involved in the accident of subsequent rescue. One notable interview was with David Sanderson, the final passenger to leave the plane and be rescued.

Couric introduced the segment with the words: "You can only imagine the fear among the passengers during those few minutes the plane was in the air and then, of course, landed in the water."

While speaking with Sanderson, who was conversing on the phone from a hospital bed, she showed sincere compassion and professionalism, ending up by commending Sanderson for checking that everyone else was off the plane before leaving himself, calling him a hero.

Of course, the most celebrated hero of that event was the captain and pilot of the flight, Captain Sully, whom Tom Hanks would later play in a major motion picture *Sully*. On February 9, 2009, Katie Couric previewed her upcoming 60 Minutes Interview with Sully, which would make her the first person to interview the pilot among the press.

Couric's Interview with Sully and Other Work on 60 Minutes

As part of Couric's work with CBS and her regular appearance as head anchor and managing editor of CBS Evening News, she also regularly contributed to the award-winning series *60 Minutes*.

On February 2, 2009, Couric opened the evening news with the words: "The crew of Flight 1549 have become national celebrities ever since their plane went down on that cold winter afternoon, two and a half weeks ago... Captain Sully, who was piloting the plane, got named a hero in his hometown of Danville, California, and, last night, a Super Bowl solute in Tampa. But Sullenberger and his crew are just now telling their harrowing accounts of that five-and-a-half-minute flight from LaGuardia airport in New York City to the Hudson River… You can see my complete interview with the captain and hew crew, Sunday evening on 60 Minutes, right here on CBS."

Without a doubt, this was one *60 Minutes* feature many across the nation did not want to miss.

For the first time, the detailed story of the flight and miraculous water landing was told from the inside. Sully and other crew members and passengers told their stories.

Sully's interview was a major hit for *60 Minutes*, and it was also a boost for Couric's career. In fact, years later, she would sit across from Tom Hanks playing Sully in the movie to reenact a portion of the interview for the movie.

Couric would contribute around six to eight stories each year to *60 Minutes* during her tenure with CBS, interviewing others such as Valerie Plame, a CIA operative whose identity was leaked to the public in 2003, eventually leading to her publishing a memoir detailing her career with the CIA and the events leading up to her resignation from the organization. Another person Couric interviewed was Robert Gates, who served as the US Secretary of defense from 2006 to 2011, and Michelle Rhee, an educator, and advocate for education reform.

Without a doubt, Couric's work with *60 Minutes* lent a good deal of seriousness to her career as a news broadcaster.

Chapter 7

The Sarah Palin Interviews

In 2008, the country was facing a difficult time. The war in Iraq was stretching on longer than anyone had initially anticipated, President Bush's decision to maintain a military presence in Iraq, looking for weapons of mass destruction, was making him increasingly unpopular.

As the United States presidential elections drew near in 2008, this war in Iraq was one of the hottest issues at hand. But the candidates on both sides had to deal with other issues, such as a crumbling US economy and the public's concerns regarding health care.

On the Democratic side, there was Barack Obama, the junior Senator from Illinois, and Joe Biden, the senior Senator from Delaware, who would later be elected President of the United States in the 2020 elections.

On the Republican side, there was John McCain, the senior Senator from Arizona, and the Governor of Alaska, Sarah Palin.

Sarah Palin—Governor, Would-Be Vice President, Author, and Reality TV Celebrity

While the public criticized John McCain for a number of reasons, including his age, Palin was a big-time personality that people either loved or loved to make fun of. She was elected the 9th governor of Alaska in 2006.

She got her start in politics when running for a City Council seat in Wasilla, Alaska. Then in 1996, she was elected mayor of that same city. Finally, after a loss as lieutenant governor of Alaska, she was elected as governor of the state in 2006. She was very popular with Alaskan voters throughout her term, even after she lost the election on the John McCain ticket.

Later, Palin would resign as governor of Alaska, write a memoir about her personal and political life, which was entitled *Going Rogue*, and even become a reality TV personality with shows such as *Sarah Palin's Alaska*, which aired on TLC.

Katie Couric Interviews Sarah Palin

In 2008, while the elections were on the horizon, Couric performed a series of interviews with Sarah Palin. Before the interviews happened, the McCain/Palin campaign was under heavy fire for lack of press access to Palin. Why have a woman candidate, the reasoning went, if you are not going to use her as a powerful voice on the ticket?

"The campaign's general strategy involved coming out with a network anchor, someone they felt had treated John well on the trail thus far," Palin would later write in her memoir regarding the idea that led to the interviews with Couric. "My suggestion was that we be consistent with that strategy and start talking to outlets like FOX and the Wall Street Journal. I really didn't have a say in which press I was going to talk to, but for some reason Nicolle seemed compelled to get me on the Katie bandwagon."

Wallace prodded Palin further, saying that Katie Couric was like her, seeing her as a working mom, which Couric was, as well. Wallace, however, argued that no such conversation ever happened. She claims she never had to cajole Palin into sitting down with Couric.

Couric recalls the situation of the interview this way: "The campaign felt they didn't want a week to go by without hearing anything from Governor Palin because they were doling out the interviews very selectively. So they decided when she was visiting some world leaders at the UN, that that would be an opportunity for her to sit down that morning and talk to me and it was very serendipitous for us, because we could— that opened the door to a lot of interesting foreign policy questions. And, also, in addition to that, the financial crisis was sort of really heating up during that week, so that was another opportunity."

Couric continues, "Then, we had scheduled an interview the following Monday, during which we were going to talk about a lot of domestic and social issues, so they gave us tremendous access."

For Couric, this was a golden opportunity at the perfect time in her career. Getting exclusive time with Palin would lead to a new door opening up to her down the road. The campaign desperately needed to hush the critics and give Palin an opportunity to speak.

Unfortunately for McCain and Palin, the interviews did not work well in their favor.

Reaction to the Interviews
In addition to airing the full 40-minute interview, CBS also divided up the content into multiple segments and dolled them out on several different formats and programs, including their morning show and the evening news.

Palin would go on to call it the "seemingly never-ending" interview and a "nine-thousand-part interview." She might have described it differently if it had not been bad for her image and the campaign in general.

For CBS, on the other hand, it meant excellent ratings. CBS Evening News gained new viewers who tuned in just to see more of the interview, and clips that were posted to YouTube were viewed millions of times.

Portions of the interview were so bad for Palin that Saturday Night Live actually performed parodies based on the clips, with Tina Fey playing Palin. Later, an official for McCain's campaign would say that Palin had not had enough time to prepare for the interview properly and that she did not have Couric's questions ahead of time.

Couric commented later on her technique, showing that she had no intention of ambushing Palin with her questions. She said, "I believe one of the reasons that the interview I conducted with Sarah Palin was so impactful is because it wasn't done through any particular ideological prism. I was so mindful of my personal affect, knowing every head tilt, expression, and follow-up question would be carefully dissected for any evidence of bias. My goal was simply to be a conduit to allow her to express her views and give those watching a chance to come to their own conclusions."

Later, Palin refused to allow Couric any more interviews, claiming that she would never waste her time with a reporter that was "obviously" so biased against her.

Meanwhile, Palin embraced the jokes made about her in some ways. She appeared herself on Saturday Night Live on more than one occasion. She also starred in the TLC series *Sarah Palin's Alaska*, which showed her and her family's life in Alaska, hunting Caribou, among other things.

Chapter 8

The Shift to Web Content

The news and news media are constantly in a state of shift. As we saw earlier in this book, the news had trouble transitioning from radio to TV in the '30s. However, live broadcasts of news events were the norm just a few years later.

Katie Couric had already established herself as a formidable figure in the world of TV. In addition to her work for CBS Evening News and *60 Minutes*, she was also involved in a series of CBS Reports, including specials such as "Children of the Recession" and "Where America Stands." She won awards such as the Columbia School of Journalism's Alfred DuPont Award for Excellence in Journalism because of her work in this series of special deep dives.

Couric also, for two seasons, had her own daytime talk show, simply called Katie.

And yet, like the news in general, she saw the need to begin a transition, including online content as part of her career repertoire.

@katiecouric

Of course, from the start of her tenure on the CBS Evening News, clips of Couric started to be available online on such places a YouTube. CBS and CBS Evening News, two distinct YouTube channels, started posting content regularly back in 2006 and have kept it up ever since.

But Katie Couric also took the internet bull by the horns in another way by hosting a one-hour internet interview program on CBSNews.com. She would go on to interview people like Vice President Al Gore, the esteemed actor, Hugh Jackman, Michelle Obama, Shakira, the hit recording artist, and New York Times columnist Thomas Friedman.

She also interviewed Ellen DeGeneres, Bill Gates, and the bestselling author Malcolm Gladwell.

This internet-only news and interview show allowed Couric to spread her wings a bit, as it were, which she would be able to do even more of in future segments of her career.

A Few Years with ABC News

Early in her career, you will recall, Katie Couric worked as a small-time reporter and anchor for ABC. Now, in 2011, she started working for that company once again. She worked as a correspondent for ABC News and worked with series like *Nightline*.

In conjunction with ABC, she also had a two-season stint as a daytime talk show host with the series *Katie*.

Then, in 2014, Couric had the opportunity to take on the world of online news once again when she transitioned from ABC to Yahoo! News.

Yahoo! News—A More Modern Take on How the News Works

Yahoo! is one of the companies born out of the DOT COM era. In 1994, Jerry Yang and David Filo established Yahoo, which provided a very different approach to internet search from that of Google. In the year 2000, it was the most popular website in the world. Yahoo got its start as a human-edited web directory. The site's original name was "Jerry and David's guide to the World Wide Web."

This concept might seem ridiculous today, in the age of algorithm-driven searches and Google Bots combing through the internet, indexing things, so we get the "best possible" results for our searches. But, in the early days of the internet, this was a surprisingly effective way to present the internet to people not familiar with it, much like a librarian makes the library much more user-friendly for readers looking for something interesting online.

Yahoo News started out as a news aggregator only. It began way back in 1996, started by Brad Clawsie. It compiled top news networks and showed people what articles were the most read and emailed.

Jumping forward to 2011, Yahoo saw the need to add original news content to the site and web service. This fits in with Yahoo's plans to become a major media organization. In 2012, Yahoo News was seen as one of the top news websites in the world.

In 2014, Yahoo News hired Couric to be the Global Anchor for the Yahoo News.

Working for Yahoo News

Couric's main contribution as Global Anchor for Yahoo News was basically to continue doing what she had been doing for years: interviewing political and celebrity figures.

Later, as Yahoo News and ABC News formed new partnerships, Couric was able to go back to contributing stories to ABC News and appear regularly on Good Morning America, taking her back to her morning show roots.

In 2017, when Verizon purchased Yahoo, Couric ended her contract and said that she would only continue to work with Yahoo on a per-project basis.

In the meantime, Couric had continued to focus on the growth of her own production company. She also started work on her tell-all memoir, *Going There*.

Looking back at an inspiring life and a successful career, Katie Couric's professionalism and dedication have been evident again and again, in her interviews, in her well-scripted introductions to difficult news items, and in her enduring smile, which she has put on day after day, even when - for one reason or another - it must have been a battle just showing up at the studio, let alone producing, on cue, the smooth and professional personality expected from her.

Made in the USA
Monee, IL
21 May 2022